Cleaning Out Grandma

How Americans Can Consume Less and Care More

Cleaning Out Grandma

How Americans Can Consume Less and Care More

Raye Lynn Husmer and Reid Husmer,
Founder of Gone for Good

Copyright ©2019
Shepherd Brands Publishing

All rights reserved.
No part of this book may be reproduced in any form or by
any electronic or mechanical means including information
storage and retrieval systems without permission, in writing.

Shepherd Brands Publishing
Greenwood Village, CO 80111
844-613-6025

ISBN-13: 978-1-7336483-0-1

Cover Artist: Bobby Morgan
Editor: Amber Wyatt
Layout Designer: Debbie Stratton, Design Dog Studio

Printed in the United States of America

Dedication

We want to dedicate our book and business to our kids. May they develop the wisdom to accumulate less stuff which will ultimately limit their physical and financial resources. Instead, may they value more principles which truly matter and which positively impact each other as well as their future communities, families, and environment.

"Don't store up treasures here on earth, where they can be eaten by moths and get rusty, and where thieves break in and steal. Store your treasures in heaven, where they will never become moth-eaten or rusty and where they will be safe from thieves. Wherever your treasure is, there your heart and thoughts will be also."

- Matt. 6:19-21 New Living Translation Bible

Contents

Preface

Once upon a time, there was a happy family that had been living in the same home for years. Like most families in the U.S., this family seemed to have acquired a lot of *stuff*. "Maybe we should buy a bigger house since we're outgrowing this one," thought the kids. "Or maybe," said the Dad, "we should go through all of this *stuff*, figure out what we really want to keep, what we can donate, and then figure out *'something else'* for what's left."

This is a story that plays out in homes across America every day and it just so happens that this is our family's story too. When we faced the daunting task of figuring out what to do with all of our *'what's left'*, we discovered that the current options in the market just weren't fitting the bill:

- Junk hauling companies that simply throw everything into a landfill;
- Donation centers with retail showrooms that only take good, usable stuff;
- And recycling centers that only take recyclables

We didn't feel good about all of our unwanted items being thrown into a landfill. Our kids, after all, will inherit all of that stuff – but not in the good way that kids usually think about inheritances!

Donation centers are great but we didn't have a truck back then. In addition, not everything we wanted to get rid of would have really been considered a treasure by someone else.

Recycling centers are a light in the darkness to keep as much stuff out of landfills as possible. Unfortunately, only a small portion of the stuff we wanted to get rid of would qualify as recyclable.

Our family needed a lot of different facilities to help deal with all of our *stuff*. We found that busy people, busy families – and especially seniors that are downsizing or transitioning to assisted living facilities – also needed a lot of different help to deal with their *stuff*. With full-time jobs, raising a family, and helping aging parents, we needed a one-stop option so that we could get all of this *stuff* dealt with, without losing our sanity. Unfortunately, that one-stop option didn't exist – until we created **Gone For Good.**

The double entendre behind the name means that items are gone for good (permanently) from homeowners' (and even business owners') locations and they are gone for good in terms of going to good causes.

As they say, *one man's trash is another man's treasure.* The question of the day for us was, "How do we turn trash into treasure?"

It's easy to throw trash in the garbage – that's where it belongs. Check!

While recycling can be tricky, there are pretty defined parameters about what can and cannot be recycled. If we stick to the rules, we can divert a lot of recyclable items that would otherwise end up in a landfill to a recycling facility. Check!

What about the good, usable stuff that other people might see as new treasures for themselves? We thought about putting it all in a retail showroom, yet we knew there were things that people wouldn't necessarily buy that would be huge blessings as donations to various local, national and international charities.

That's it…we'll partner with charities to pay it forward. Check!

We liked the idea of a resale shop and people love the thrill of the hunt. We decided that a thrift store made the most sense for good, usable items that could be repurposed. Check!

By creating **Gone For Good,** we solved our own problem – well, not that day we didn't, but we now have a go-to option for our family's future clean-out adventures. What we found is that other families who were in the same boat that our family was in, were thrilled to find a simple resource that took away much of the hassle and headaches associated with *Cleaning Out Grandma*. We also found that even though people were willing to part with items they no longer wanted, it mattered a lot to them where their items ended up. They loved the idea of indirectly being able to donate to charities and knowing that their once-treasured items would be enjoyed by someone else in the years to come.

It's funny that people will keep stuff in their homes for years and years but once they decide they want something gone, they want it gone NOW. When adult children are helping their parents transition into new living quarters – often doing so from an out-of-state location – time is always of the essence. We wanted **Gone For Good** to help as many people as possible and leave the lightest footprint on the planet. That's a huge goal! How were we ever going to be able to do that? Franchising! We are proud that **Gone For Good** launched its franchise efforts in mid-2019. With a solid business model, a passionate team, and entrepreneurs who resonate with our mission, we hope to be in a town near you very soon.

Reid and Raye Lynn Husmer
Founders
Gone For Good
GoneForGoodStore.com

Part I:
Look Into a Lifestyle Lift

A Solely Self-Centered Start
is at Least a Start

"I don't think you're getting the point of this exercise."

CHAPTER 1:

Should it Stay or Should it Go?

Too many dishes, not enough cabinets

OJ in a Wine Glass

When Darla and her husband Dave retired and decided to downsize from a 7,000 sq. ft. home to a 2,000 sq. ft. home, she had questions. None of them, however, were more pressing than the question: *What should I take with me?* In the end, she took everything, as most of us do. What's the matter with this? Well, as we all learned in our first science class, anything that has mass is matter. In our industry, when there's more matter than space, amassment occurs. In layman's terms, a collection of unnecessary clutter accumulates where the space needed is not available.

So, what do you suppose happened when Darla dared to take dozens of boxes from her old home to her new home? To say the least, unpacking only further complicated her life. She started by filling her new cupboards to the limit with wine glasses and carafes. When it came time for her to unpack juice glasses there was no space left for them! Darla decided to invite a friend over for breakfast and discuss her options on the unpacking dilemma.

When Darla reached into her new cupboards for glasses to pour their orange juice in, she was confronted with the root of all her frustrations.

"All I can offer you is OJ in a wine glass!" she shrieked.

Her friend glanced around the room at all the glasses scattered about countertops and realized, the cupboards were completely full. While trying to determine how to help, she accepted the OJ in its long, delicate vessel and ventured,

"Darla, I'm sorry but something is bugging me above all else, I didn't think the two of you drank."

Darla glanced about, "We don't, but this box of entertaining wares was unpacked first and now there's no room for the juice glasses! All that's available are glasses for the scads of people we can no longer entertain in this tiny space."

Had Darla only determined what should stay and what should go before her move, perhaps she and her friend would have quickly unpacked and been able to enjoy a traditional glass of OJ at breakfast followed by a match of tennis, a much more enjoyable morning. Or should I say, repacked? That's right, directly after Darla and her friend determined the many oversights that occurred with her move, they spent the remainder of the day repacking unneeded items to make room for the things she and her husband actually needed.

If you think Dave and Darla are a unique unit, I urge you to reconsider. According to an article from the *New York Post,* the average American has at least 23 useless items taking up space in their homes. The same article quotes a survey by Closet Maid, the worldwide leader in home storage, that 57% of Americans have a hard time getting rid of things because they are sentimental.

"The kids refer to my storage unit as the Smithsonian. I have encyclopedias, VHS tapes, floppy disks, and college mementos."

It is something we see all too often, many people are distraught by imagining permanent separation from something they may find useful in the future or something that is a reminder of the past.

Just like Darla and Dave, Norma began a nomadic trek to the land of milk and honey. Seniors refer to this place as the retirement community. Instead of calling her gal pal, Norma solicited the help of her daughter-in-law, Robin, an employee with Senior on the Move. Unlike Darla and Dave, Norma began discarding items before her move. Unfortunately, she encountered many of the same dilemmas the couple did as she made the decision of what to keep and what to toss. At the crux of every decision, she found herself pondering many outcomes. *How can I abandon this family heirloom? What if I get rid of this and end up needing it later? This was a gift! What if the giver realizes I just gave it away?*

Looms are more common than you would think

From the concerns Norma had, you may have already realized what she couldn't, it's seldom about the thing but about the feeling the thing elicits. Over the years, we've seen more things, more than we could think to recall, and there are a diversity of reasons which make each special. Sometimes the things are all we have left of someone. Sometimes the things have a lot of monetary value. Sometimes the things are as unique as the individuals who we obtain them from. What has never been unique are the many reasons that keep us from tossing them out. The most common reasons are:

- Sentiment

- Uncertainty

- Relational Attachment

Like Norma, you all have those special, sentimental items. It's no secret that items like that are difficult to let go of. Truthfully, as common as sentiment is, often times there is a thin line between healthy and unhealthy habits pertaining to it. Try writing about the sentiment attached to the item. What are the memories that the item evokes? Remember the energy that you it gives you. You will find that the journal you keep for your beloved items takes up less space than storing it for another decade. By writing about the items, you can reminisce as frequently as you'd like and easily transport or store them in a way you never could before.

If you're uncertain of an item's usefulness, it probably isn't worth as much as you think. To eliminate uncertainty start by listing items to determine how often they are used. Visualize the relevance of each item to establish its worth according to its use in your household. Many people fear that a 30% off item they are not using today will become useful in the coming years.

Meanwhile, the bargain is the space needed to store something that's actually, consistently used. By giving yourself more space for the items you are using today, you will gain peace of mind.

Relational attachment occurs when a loved one is distant or has passed. This is a product of the fear that you will lose the memories of a person if you lose the items associated with them. Loss is inevitable, but accepting this is a very important component of the grieving process. Moving on emotionally means getting rid of items like Kris has to do later in the book. Kris realized that her attachment to the relationship was the actual reality causing interference as she purged, not the actual items (pins) she sorted through. In the end she discovered the attachment she had to her mother's pins wasn't as significant as her attachment to her mother.

Before *you* get too attached to things or the memories associated with them, let me explain what happens when inanimate objects are allowed to influence your decisions. Ultimately, you keep things you don't need and accumulate more than you can hold. By teaching people why they

These old synthetic Christmas trees are a great donation item

accumulate items in the first place, Gone for Good can create some detachment to those feelings, feelings which are often disguised by a cold, hard transaction. You see, amassment equates to an ownership issue. From the time you are small, you are familiarized with a society that opens their clutches to purchase a barrage of gifts, decorations, all of the latest fads and more. An attachment to things forms, and subsequently, the feeling of possession forms.

In some cases, personal attachment progresses to a ritualistic form of collecting items regardless of their value. This is a disorder known as hoarding and over 5% of the world's population struggles with it. Some people have experienced such profound loss, they can not conceive letting anything go. I cannot emphasize enough how deeply we become attached to things but I will discuss this in greater length later.

As you propel through annual celebrations, earning incomes that facilitate accumulation, your grasp on things begins to tighten. You strengthen the idea that you are superior for having more. Nigel Marsh is a management and communication specialist that speaks and writes on excessive consumption. "There are thousands and thousands of people out there leading lives of quiet, screaming desperation, where they work long, hard hours at jobs they hate to enable them to buy things they don't need to impress people they don't like."[1] For the cost of societal acceptance, it's no wonder we don't want to give anything up.

Evaluating the True Cost

Not only do you hold on to everything, but you buy bigger homes in the name of fortifying the things within larger quarters. Hallmarks of success become the burden of assets. The assets, may I remind you, have you packing and repacking when you need to move and let them go more than ever. What you really need to do, is to remove the blinders from your eyes and truly face the obstacles of ownership. Only then can you begin to evaluate the true cost of stuff.

In fact, evaluating the true cost of items is the key to deciding what should stay and what should go. Evaluating things in this manner requires a more abstract approach than simply attaching dollars-and-cents worth to what we see. Einstein discovered that space and time are interwoven in relativity and just the same, Gone for Good has discovered space and time are part of our substance as a society. So much so, that they are the key components we urge customers to evaluate as they decide what to keep and what to discard. The gravity of this discovery revolutionized our industry. The process comes down to these *basic questions about each item:*

Is there space for it?

- Do you have the mental space and physical space available for the item?

- This decision should be characterized by your ability to recall and find it.

- Consider your age, researchers suggest seniors minimize belongings due to a decline in memory.

Is there time for it?

- Is the required time commitment for the item in question proportionate to its cost?

- This decision is characterized by the time you spend with it.

- If the cost to purchase, store, and maintain an item exceeds the time you use it, you should let it go.

Let's explore each of these strategies more in-depth.

Mrs. Riley packed her class with the best teaching components money could buy. She stocked her shelves with literature for every subject. In each corner were components of creative projects for every lesson. While they were organized very well, she found difficulty applying the new material to her curriculum. The excess of new books, games, and lessons led her back to the same ways she had always taught. She had so much stuff to incorporate into her lessons, it simply wasn't possible. Mrs. Riley kept accumulating until finally, she couldn't even remember everything she had. Drawing from the recesses of her mind, she only used cataloged and accessible items.

If she'd understood the principle of how physical space collaborates with mental space to start with, using Gone for Good to purge outdated curriculum material instead of purchasing new replacements could have saved a lot of time and money. Nevertheless, we carted away expensive material that she never used. Perhaps the greatest value Mrs. Riley could have uncovered here, would have been more time to actually implement something new.

Here is an example of a collection that doesn't allow enough space to track items physically or mentally. There is no way to mentally keep a catalog of this many games. If you're facing this scenario, keep your favorites and donate the rest to your local youth center.

Not understanding this element of decluttering is the very reason many of us wear the same few outfits over and over. Despite having closets laden with different designs and styles, we often wear the first thing that comes to mind. Sure, we may like the way a particular cozy sweater feels or the way a pair of jeans fit, but instant recall wins every time. We know that in a society bursting with responsibilities, more obligations crowd your brains than anything. This keeps you rotating through two dozen outfits, that is, unless you are a Kardashian. After all, isn't it more time that we are all after? So time should definitely be an essential factor in your discussions about whether something stays or go.

A young man named Richard dreamt of getting a motorcycle for years. When he was at an auction and one came up, he had to bid on it, and wouldn't you know, he won the highest bid. You might have thought his greatest obstacle to enjoying this new purchase now, was his wife. What really kept him from enjoying the bike was the monthly maintenance required to keep it humming smoothly. Oh yeah, and the monthly insurance premiums dampened his enthusiasm. In addition to all the costs, he spent the limited time he had on weekends going to and from the shop for repairs. In the end, the cost of the motorcycle was greater than Richard's love for it.

The Liberty of Getting Rid of an Item

Many families collect Christmas decor to rival their neighbors. Needless to say, large spaces are required to house the annual competition you add to each year. You spend almost as much time storing and stacking your splendors as you do displaying them.

Nancy made it her duty to assemble an adorned tree in every room of her home. Each tree had a different theme. Her

Gone for Good often needs an entire room to display discarded Christmas items

daughter's tree was ballet-themed, with tiny slippers and tutus draped on every tier. Her son's tree regaled his hearty support of all things athletic, with pennants perched on every limb. The themes amused her until she realized the season made for a mighty mess post-production. The time it cost her to deck the halls was just too much. Finally, in her most ardent display of holiday goodwill, she donated each ornament, wreath and tree to Gone for Good.

Remember Norma from earlier in our story? Although her daughter-in-law, Robin, was able to keep her from packing up too many senseless items, she was not able to evade the

KitchenAid. Yes, you know it, the $400 mixer brigades of brides are purchasing. It's a hot item that holds as much allure to a 75-year-old woman as a newly endowed housewife. In Norma's own words, "It's how I make my world-famous cinnamon rolls!"

Robin understood Norma's thoughts around the KitchenAid. It was her sense of identity. Thoughts are a formidable opponent to all, even to a seasoned senior mover. That KitchenAid was packed and unpacked. Time passed and during one visit from Robin, Norma noted her eyes resting on a very dusty KitchenAid in the corner. Making eye contact they laughed. "Hey!" Robin said, "You've been here four months, and I've yet to enjoy one cinnamon roll."

Yes, the burden of proof rests in pastry here. Norma had to admit, she simply did not need as much as she thought she did. Norma defined herself with the KitchenAid. Once she realized she did not need it to be a good nana, or mother, or neighbor it became much easier for her to let it go. ❖

CHAPTER 2:

The Racoon in the Freezer

The Downside to Downsizing

You may recall a rather rose-colored-glow on downsizing in Chapter 1. After all, if you have a friend like Darla's or a daughter-in-law like Norma's, you're motivated to purge. For many people, igniting their own willpower to start the process and fully commit to its completion is tough. Even if they feel inclined to pack, they must sort and discard. More often than not, this kind of responsibility rests with one person who is biased, making it harder to determine what should stay and what should go.

Remember the notion that sole ownership creates strong attachment? If you're solely responsible for determining the true value of each and every item, you may not be as objective as a team would be. Again, detachment is key. A crew such as ours can come in and see a teacup for what it is: a small vessel equipped to contain a hot beverage. To one woman, Irene, a teacup was, "A small representation of the class and sophistication our culture has lost over time." Therefore, each pint-sized china cup she owned seemed more valuable to her than anything. Irene simply wanted to hold onto a time in space where she felt more comfortable and content.

When you experience difficulties discarding items like teacups, downsizing screeches to an alarming halt. More often than not, items, seen as relics of the past, become much too important not to keep. In the case of Irene, frustration and resentment occurred after a seemingly quick job turned out to require much more time than anticipated. As anyone who has assisted in a similar situation would tell you, the greatest frustration occurs from the energy it takes to engage with someone who rationalizes keeping any and everything. Irene's helpers listened to constant lectures on the significance of every item on her shelves when their mere existence wasn't relevant or pertinent to the helpers. They were simply trying to give their time, as a valuable commodity.

As they made progress throughout the day, more time slipped away. Everything the helpers started to box for hauling, Irene pulled back out. Suddenly she had the stage, detailing who gave it to her, when they gave it to her, and why they gave it to her. According to her reasoning, if her brother gave her a matchbox back in 1947, she should keep it in loving memory of their relationship forever. It's no wonder that when her team got ready to move to the cold, dark basement, they feared what they would uncover. After all, if items showcased in the light of day couldn't easily be determined as 'stayers' or 'goers', what kind of things would be pulled and pondered from the dark catacombs beneath?

There was no way of knowing what they would uncover that day, even if their suspicions alerted them to the reality that Irene kept things she shouldn't. Leery and long-ago-exhausted, they made their way through the basement, quickly discovering corners and crevices encased in cobwebs and covered with boxes and bags. Like so many, Irene also had a freezer stocked with enough frozen overflow to feed an army. After it was unplugged and thawed, its contents began the slow excavation from a mixture of ice and slush. In this process, a block of something altogether bizarre melted to reveal the most unlikely freezer inhabitant of all, a raccoon.

Logic and objection are sometimes concepts as foreign in the mind of a downsizer as a raccoon in a freezer. In cases like Irene's, fear pervades as she attempts to toss stuff. As with most people, the source of her fear was permanent loss. Evidently, even the pelt or meat or goodness-knows-what of a raccoon was significant enough to evoke this fear. With such a conundrum in place, I determine that there is, in fact, a downside to downsizing: We're all a little bit hoardy, because we're human, because we feel and become attached to things. The struggle that accompanies this fear is ultimately inevitable.

Don Aslett is an author of numerous books on decluttering and personal organization. Aslett describes the downside too. "I've discovered something interesting: Clutter is probably the only thing on Earth that's truly democratic. It doesn't discriminate for race, creed, color, IQ, or economic status. And male and female are equally guilty—although it does seem clear from more than forty years of professional cleaning and all the confessions that have been sent to me that men seem to go for bigger, more expensive junk; women are somewhat ahead in creative excuses. Other than that, it's dead even!"

Irene's move and clutter's pervasiveness teaches us two very important lessons that keep us on track today, helping us concentrate more on the upside to downsizing. I believe these two concepts are helpful to any individual or team helping rid of items:

1. Never let the attached party dictate the removal and packing process without objective feedback.

2. Assume more will be removed than first regarded; the Out of Sight Out of Mind principle usually prevails when purging.

The Objective Onslaught

Aslett, the decreer of democratic clutter, further explains why it's so darn easy to keep adding to your stuff, "The second you give it a second thought, it's going to get a second chance." It's so helpful to have at least one person beside you to sort through it and decide not to keep it. All jokes aside, if a team with the same objective isn't put together to tackle the project, very little headway can be made.

On-the-other-hand, when a team is working together, even the most simple concepts coincide to create a more manageable perspective. For example, the team of two golden-age, garden-gurus Gertie and Gwen. Each prized their perennials, pots, and posies with persistent esteem. When it came time for Gertie to move and clear her garden shed, it was only natural she asked her fellow garden enthusiast, Gwen, to assist with the clean-out.

When Gertie just couldn't decide what to let go of, Gwen was right there to assist, asking questions like:

• *"Has the shelf-life of these perennial bulbs expired?"*

• *"Has this old pot lost its value?"*

- *"Are you planning on potting a few posies at Paradise Manor, or is it not worth your time?"*

The questions made it easier for Gertie to gauge what was worth keeping, but even then, she had difficulty. She amassed quite the collection of inscribed watering cans, all prizes for the years she won 'garden of the year' in her neighborhood. They were a great source of pride to her, so it's no wonder she struggled with the idea of parting with them. Luckily, Gwen stepped in to reassure her and to redirect her thoughts, "Gertie, darling, do you really need all of them? Isn't there one which is more special than the others?" Suddenly she remembered, there was! Many years back, Gertie's late husband inscribed his own special message on one of the cans the year of their 25th wedding anniversary. Gertie very quickly decided that if she could only keep one, that would certainly be the one she kept. She displayed it proudly at Paradise Manor, in her sight, and on her mind for all the right reasons.

Raid your garden shed, cupboards, and shelves—
we rarely need more than one of the same functional item

Out of Sight, Out of Mind

Here's the truth. When we keep things out of sight and out of mind for too long, we rarely have any reasons for keeping them. Case-in-point, Irene.

I really think Irene would have mentioned the raccoon in her freezer if she'd even remembered it was there. It's the kind of thing, like smelly socks or crusty dishes, that you try to hide when company comes. She didn't remember it though, for the simple reason that it was buried in ice. Think about it, the only reason a dog can find his buried bone is by the scent of it. If the raccoon had been given much more time to thaw, it's likely the stench would have alerted Irene and her team that something demanded attention. That's what stuff, particularly buried stuff, has a way of doing: turning into a problem too unreasonable not to be resolved.

While it seems simple to some and impossible to others, it's best to keep useful items at eye-level where they're easy to grab. Mentioned earlier was the futility in amassing a packed closet. While the point was to prove humans can never seem to sift through all of their clothing to give each an ample wear, the point now is that closets seem to be among the worst culprits when it comes to keeping things out of mind. Several closets come to mind that have been totally stuffed rod-to-rod, floor-to-ceiling. There was no way the purveyors of such plunder could ever utilize all the shoes and sweaters stacked sky-high. In many of these cases, boxes of shoes become additional shelving.

In the same way, every drawer can become a junk drawer if not properly monitored which begs the point: if it doesn't fit, why is it being kept? At this point, we might recommend all sorts of approaches to drum down drawers. One of our favorites, the

"I started purging stuff in the junk drawer and got carried away."

Marie Kondo method, helps to tidy and toss simultaneously. If you require baby steps to pare down possessions, Aslett has an approach that takes us right back to the drawer. That's right, if you focus on one drawer, you may realize how helpful it is to ponder items usefulness than to suddenly trash them. Aslett's tactic is more passive, "Ninety-nine percent of what ends up clutter and litter in a home is stuff we carry through the door and don't have an immediate use or place for... One way to keep a grip on all this is a box or drawer where you can put all the in-transit or undecided the minute you come in, then you have it contained and controlled. It can stay in there while you decide where it goes or until you use it. This is kind of improved junk drawer."

Whether you can muster the immediate courage to dismantle a closet or dejunk a drawer, or it takes you a few attempts, the point is to start. Grab someone. Ask their opinion if yours is too clouded. Bring what is out of sight to light. Bring it to the forefront of your mind by exposing your shelves, closets, and dare I say it, freezer. ❖

*When we bury things, we lose them. We also lose the ability
to recall what's there or what the room looked like beforehand.
We're then unable to use either the items or the space.*

CHAPTER 3:

The Psychology of Evaluating Ourselves Before Our Stuff

The Casualties of Battle

After reading the last chapter, I hope that something resonated with you in a way that you are now resolved to go forth and conquer! As Kathi Lipp, a seasoned, serial, simplifier-of-space cautions, "We can buy organizing books, download the charts, and resolve to get rid of clutter. But if we don't attack the heart of the issue—the **fear, guilt, and shame** in our lives that cause us to buy what we don't really need—we are going to use that clutter to build our own prisons and keep us from connecting with others."

Aslett also paints a bleak picture, wagering the counter argument that we are not passively captive to clutter but in an active war to recapture ourselves instead, all the while assaulting the rooted feelings and things we've allowed to take residency with us. "So much of human history seems to be a struggle to get out of bondage—captivity to some country, city, race, or nation. Many a life and limb has been lost fighting for rights and freedoms—for release, so we can get out and get on with living and enjoy life. We, of course, blame most bondage on 'them'—the leaders, the government, the organization, the Lord, the society, the terrorists. Seldom ourselves; we're just the helpless victims. That might be so 10 percent of the time, but the other 90 percent is all our own personal bondage or unhappiness. The situation is self-inflicted. We hold our own feet to the fire; our situation is what we make it or allow it to be. We could use those same feet to walk away. When it comes to clutter, we are at the root of most of what we're buried in right now. We allowed or even invited it (generally paid for it, too) to inundate us."

Still, there are two types of 'we' referred to above. You see, this war takes different casualties:

- Those who are dealing with some heart issues, served by an objective buddy or benefactor, like those mentioned in chapter 2.

- Those who are alone and struggle to seek professional intervention.

Those with a Heart Issue

The process of helping the first type of casualty is much easier but no less painful. After all, getting at a heart issue is much easier than getting at a hard issue such as OCD, dementia or schizophrenia. To show how a heart issue is recognized as part of a process, let's revisit Darla.

A box of entertaining wares were an early demise for Darla as she unpacked in her new home. Having no sentimental attachment to them, she disposed of the wine glasses early into unpacking. It was another box of entertainment ware that was the problem. The contents she could not so easily dispose of, and the simple reason was a heart issue, which came packed as neatly as the dishes in it.

If you or I had unpacked these dishes they would have looked like any other. To Darla, these dishes were her mother's entertaining flatware. While her mother had been gone a very long time, the memories of her and the lavish parties she threw, were as alive in Darla's mind as Darla herself. Her objective friend, sipping OJ and setting aside items to discard, would not have been able to see those memories or even appreciate them as

Darla did. However, one thing emerged that her friend clearly saw, a heart issue.

> **Fear**—Afraid of losing more of her mother, Darla found it difficult to part with her dishes. So often people rationalize keeping something because they are afraid of losing something else. Their only way to overcome such a fear is often through the lens of someone objective who can separate the intangible feeling from the tangible item.

Thankfully, Darla had a friend, and just as she discarded her wine glasses, the flatware was next to follow.

A woman named Kay, who was much like Darla, similarly packed unused dishes. Kay found her dishes difficult to discard because her mother-in-law had given them to her as a wedding gift. Kay could still hear her, "These are a family heirloom. Please take good care of them." How then, Kay thought, would getting rid of them remotely resemble taking care of them? Grappling with the weight of her thoughts, she had an obvious heart issue.

> **Guilt**—Tormented by thoughts of her mother-in-law's expectations, Kay had spent her whole life tip-toeing around the heirlooms. In fact, she was so afraid of damaging them, she hadn't even unpacked them yet.

Despite tip-toeing around everything, especially that particular box of china, every piece broke in the final move, providing Kay with a reminder that even though we're careful, things are never certain.

What was certain to Kate, struggling with purging dishes, was her abundant wealth. The wealth that enabled her to amass not one but five sets of very nice dishes. Furthermore, she was certain that getting rid of them would be proof that she was somehow ungrateful or unaware of how well she had it. She had not always had it so well, you know. Kate felt duty-bound to remember that. Her heart issue was as old as she was.

Shame—Flooded by memories of her lowly start and status, Kate couldn't part with anything, especially items in abundance. If being grateful and cognizant of her improved position meant holding on to items for dear life, she was going to do it. Even when her friend suggested becoming a benefactor to the less fortunate, Kate's shame kept her anchored to her resolve, insisting that she help the less fortunate in a different way.

Kate died with her dishes. When Gone for Good came to clear out her house, per her five children's requests, not one of them asked to keep even a set. They were comfortable with their own wealth and how it supported their individuality. Anything that belonged to Kate, died with her, including her feelings of shame that kept her from truly enjoying life for the decades she was trapped by her belongings.

Those with a Hard Issue

Sometimes life presents people with problems that prevent enjoyment no matter how much they want it. For some people, fear gives way to anxiety, guilt, obsessive thoughts, shame, and forms of self-harm. Left unresolved, scenarios far more sinister than dish-dilemmas occur. These hard issues sometimes become the foundation for a hoarding disorder.

According to Dr. Gregory L. Jantz, Ph. D., the founder of The Center • A Place of HOPE in Edmonds, Washington, "The main determiner of whether a behavior is just a personal preference or a disorder usually has to do with whether or not, and how much, that behavior has begun to negatively impact daily functioning." Dr. Jantz also provided the generally recognized symptoms of hoarding from the Mayo Clinic:

- Cluttered living spaces
- Inability to discard items
- Keeping stacks of newspapers, magazines, or junk mail
- Moving items from one pile to another without discarding anything
- Acquiring unneeded or seemingly useless items, including trash
- Difficulty managing daily activities, procrastinating big decisions

- Difficulty organizing items

- Perfectionism

- Excessive attachment to possessions and discomfort letting others touch or borrow possessions

- Limited or no social interactions

Hoarding is often a difficult issue that extends from floor to ceiling

As a word of caution, if you or a loved one exhibit any of these tendencies, please seek help. When things progress to this very severe form of consumption and collection, these people— people who experienced such profound loss—cannot conceive letting go of anything. Hauling services like ours, although formed of very productive and well-meaning people, can't always help; instead, services like Bio-One must be solicited, as they are equipped to handle the hazardous waste that often accompanies hoarding. Separate counseling input is strongly suggested as well.

When you have dealt with hoarding, images stay seared into your memory that provide the best explanation of the hard issue. While hoarding is a hard issue, it points to a strong conclusion that, deep within us, the issue at heart is really unresolved emotions which construct, nurture, and compound our desire to hold on to things. Draw up a plan, circle the wagons, and take no prisoners! Otherwise, it's likely that you will become a prisoner of your stuff. ❖

"I'm going to be overwhelmed until Gone for Good comes on Monday to set me up."

Part II:
Create a Conscious Conscience

An Awakening to
How Our Stuff Impacts Others
Shifts Us Out of a Self-Centered Mode
to a Positive-Impact Mode

CHAPTER 4:

How to Begin
When You're at the End

Stuck in the Past

Something you dismiss more than downsizing is death. That is because the finality of our ending is as disheartening to many as the finality occurring when they dispose of personal items. More often than not, you want to live forever, and you want our stuff to have as fortunate a fate. If you've dealt with heart issues, a more balanced perspective initiates a more realistic conclusion though. Stuff is just stuff. Remembering the stories behind the stuff makes the people in them immortal.

Kris was struggling to get rid of her deceased mother's items when she quite literally got stuck. When it came to analyzing the value of her mother's pin box. She uncovered it in a very large armoire in her mother's bedroom, and when she opened the box to reveal the contents to a friend, she found more than just jewelry encased by blue velvet lining. She found memories associated with each pinprick. As she turned them over and over to her friend and fellow admirer, they poked her again and again, and not just in a way that stung, but in a way that stayed. Each revealed a special time or occasion for her late mother, Geraldine.

There was the very first one Geraldine received as a child and the very last she received from her late husband. Everyone was beautiful and unique, so a struggle ensued when Kris vocalized, "I think I will keep and display them all."

"Display them?" her friend Susan remarked, "How will you do that?"

"Well, I don't know, but they all meant so much to my mother," Kris points out.

"What do they mean to *you?*" Susan quipped.

"Well, that one my father gave her. He slipped on the ice and broke his tailbone bringing it home to her one frigid Christmas Eve. When he presented it to her, the two laughed and laughed."

"You know," Susan started, "Your mother isn't here to relive that Christmas memory every time she puts it on anymore. Unless you want to wear it to revisit the story in a similar way, I suggest getting rid of it. Write down the story so you don't forget, but, I don't think you will."

With that reasoning, Kris packaged the pins in a neat parcel and headed to the local, vintage consignment shop where her mom used to shop religiously. After exchanging formal hellos with the shop's owner, a good friend of her mother's, Kris got right to the business of selling the pins. Before she reached the door, she noticed stacks of sweaters lining a shelved-wall. "You know," she said to the owner who had began to admire and price her pins.

"I have an armoire that would look great in that corner. I noticed you have an overflow of sweaters. They would look so pretty stacked in its shelving, those scarves draped over the open doors." Kris said pointing to an array of brightly colored, silk bunched in another corner.

"How much?" the owner replied, more than a little skeptical. "It's free to you. It belonged to my mother and this was her favorite store for shopping. I'd love for a little bit of her to be here."

With that good gesture, Kris said goodbye to her mom's favorite shop and the respective owner. You see death is all about saying goodbye. If Geraldine had learned to say goodbye when she was living, Kris wouldn't have had to do it for her after she died. Getting people to realize and to relate to this concept of goodbye is important. Margareta Magnusson, a self-described "death cleaner" said it best in *The Gentle Art of Swedish Death Cleaning:*

> "Do not ever imagine that anyone will wish—or be able— to schedule time off to take care of what you didn't bother to care of yourself. No matter how much they love you, don't leave this burden to them."

Stuff is a burden in as much a way as the thing which ultimately ends our life. Similarly, even though its days aren't necessarily numbered, things have a life cycle too, one that can revolve in a way ours can't. If its revolution is handled appropriately, it can actually signify a new beginning of some sort. If we don't get stuck in the past.

Marooned on Memory Lane

I started his hauling company after moving numerous times. Each time I discovered boxed items transported from house to house, that had never been opened. I realized I was just moving stuff because I had space for it with no logical reason to keep it. I needed to start unloading items in the most responsible way possible. The solution came when I dissected my belongings into piles to keep and discard. Like most novice movers, I was getting stuck early in the process.

You see, even when I objectively determined the true value of an item by determining if it cost too much time or space, I would get derailed from discarding when I thought about how many of the items held significant memories. Even though they were no longer useful, they were representations of my son's childhood.

I had difficulty permanently parting with items like a toddler car bed, big building blocks, and a chair now too small for him.

Items like toddler bed are designed for specific times and purposes,
so be mindful of those when it's time to donate

In the process of feeling stuck about these items, I realized that their true value came from the memories associated with them. I took a few pictures, for memory sake, and gave them to a neighbor whose son was just the right age to enjoy them.

Would Reid's son appreciate this toddler chair
when he becomes an adolescent boy?

Taking a picture is a far better way of remembering significant memories than holding on to every item that elicits a feeling. The memories can also be a hang-up for movers, particularly to those trying to make new beginnings at their impending ends. The silver-haired sect may recognize that life continues in a more tangible way if unused collections of stuff don't remain in storage.

They value their introduction to more worthwhile callings, charity, recycling, however, feelings of nostalgia block progress in much the same way it did for Reid. When they eventually start to sort out their piles, it's not their child's growth and change that astounds them most. No, most generally it's coming to terms with their own mortality, which may halt processes before they've even begun. And if caretakers come along after they are gone, cleaning up what the deceased couldn't, they too will find that pictures can just as easily stall their progress.

When on memory lane, move past the common road traps. Begin sorting items that have less intimacy attached to them. Classic clutter-creatures are amazed when they get rid of objects like furniture filled with tchotchkes, boxes of old clothing, and shelves of books. They see how much easier it is to uncover objects of value. Remember Kris from the beginning of the story?

Determined to get rid of the armoire in addition to the pins, she went straight home from the vintage shop and began emptying the armoire of its contents. It was brimming with old clothes that Kris neither wanted or fit into. She bagged them up for the clothing drive her church was having. When it was mostly empty, she surveyed its bare shelves and drawers. That's when she saw another box. She opened it slowly. Inside were black and white photos of her father's and mother's honeymoon. Would she keep them? The thought crossed her mind that their significance might be lost.

The point is: She didn't have to look at them and decide that immediately. All kinds of feelings could have been stirred up if she had tried without pondering, halting her progress altogether. Instead, she put the lid back on the box and slipped it into her tote. Then, with renewed vigor, she opened the doors adjacent to her mother's.

They were that of her father's armoire, and she knew, items encountered there-in might have significance only pertaining to him. At another time she could determine that. Right then, she excelled full speed ahead, unattached and determined not to get marooned on memory lane.

Always Aware

In this chapter, I've talked about the difficulties that come along with death because it reminds us that everything has an expiration date. Meaning, even if a person passes and in turn passes their stuff along, it no longer belongs to them. That is why I must refer back to that sweet woman, Margareta Magnusson, who coined the term death cleaning as an artform. Perhaps she does this, because of her radical idea that we should always be in a state of awareness related to her things.

Here's the most radical part, it's an idea applicable to everyone. After all, none of us know when we will die, but we can be certain we will. If we constantly entertained the notion that we're going to die, maybe we should show attention to the notion that we're not taking a single earthly possession with us. This really speaks once more to the ownership issues I addressed supporting the far-reaching impact.

If you begin to see the cost of accumulation and the wisdom in scaling down as you age, the benefits are untold. Magnusson shared a sweet story about her mother-in-law who seemed to grasp this concept in a way few do. She told how her mother-in-law would periodically give family, including her, dishes and linens they admired. More importantly, she gave them away while she was still alive, knowing someday they would no longer belong to her. She wanted to make sure their next home was the right one. You see, she recognized the life cycle of her items, that they would and should evolve just as she was. As she needed less, she gave away more. ❖

> # The space in which we live should be for the person we are becoming now, not for the person we were in the past.
>
> **-Marie Kondo**

CHAPTER 5:

Circulate Life and Charity

*Geoff and the warehouse donation center
for the nonprofit "A Precious Child"*

When in Doubt, Donate!

So now, even though you may feel more comfortable with the idea of awareness and letting go, your path of discarding may not be as clear-cut. You may clearly feel a sense of responsibility to circulate life but don't know how to do it. Gone for Good prides itself in being that compass to confused and clutter-stricken clients, suggesting three avenues of removal—reduce, resell, and recycle. There is a reason why donations are the first and primary form of reduction covered in this book. Up until now, we've helped you decide what to get rid of but have been relatively quiet, about what to do with it once you've definitely decided not to keep it. With that realization, we heartily hark, when in doubt, donate!

If you don't believe us, listen to what self-professed decluttering expert, Dana K. White, says in her book *Decluttering at the Speed of Life*. "I have done it all. I have milked every dollar out of my stuff by selling it on eBay. I've sold it on Craigslist and through Facebook groups. I've been a member of Freecycle

"We haven't parked our cars in there since the summer of 2006."

(a group where you are only allowed to give things away for free), and I've held multiple garage sales in one year … As I shifted into the mode of fast and furious decluttering, I began selling less and donating more. And once I stopped worrying about how much money I could get for things, I started making major progress."

Yes, sometimes it's nice to have additional income from selling items. This is something we participate in through the format of our thrift-store; however, if you value time above other commodities, donating is the way to go.

Both the thrift store and warehouse work with over 21 non profit organizations around Denver. Often times, the items collected are donated. This past summer we donated to victims of the Westbury Apartment fires. Amanda was caring for her

David Camit helps a family load their newly-donated couch
at the Gone for Good warehouse

ill father in their apartment when they lost everything. Gone for Good used furniture and household items to furnish the family's new space.

In the winter we were introduced to an Army veteran. Delecia had traveled to Colorado from Louisiana after an injury in Iraq to start a new life. It was much harder to survive than she could have anticipated, especially with six kids. After she found an apartment Gone for Good helped out with the furniture.

Think about the many processes embarked upon by White and so many like her. I know for certain that a part-time employee is required to handle eBay items exclusively. Gone for Good's first eBay prodigy, Barb, accepted the position after aligning time and space to accumulate items we brought to her. In the process of selling items, she had to simultaneously be ready to ship and relocate said items. It's a rotating, profitable process and requires a unique individual to adhere to its strict cycle. That's why some purgers, picking this path first, get derailed. In the end, items and/or money don't circulate with the intended fervor at the beginning of a disposal process.

Barb Johnsen, Ebay resale expert for Gone for Good

A more relatable but undeniably similar process and outcome pertain to the good, old-fashioned American garage sale. How many people do you know who set up, line, and price items in their garage only to never sell all of them or move them from that space again? Or, how many people do you know who get hung-up on haggling at their garage sale, only to lose a prospective buyer?

I know from personal experience, that haggling sometimes completely halts a sell along with the resolve to get rid of something. I had a nice pair of boots that I hadn't really intended on purchasing, but somehow they mysteriously appeared in my closet. So, I decided to make that money back by listing them for sale. Keep in mind, I wasn't going to accept one dollar less than what I'd paid. To most people browsing that group, my price seemed unreasonable. Instead of relenting and selling them for less, I took down the listing and put up my feet, squarely fashioning those boots on each. Despite a fashionable-gain, I was actually out money and time. As time passed, the boots' relation to current fashion standards became quite questionable, so much so that I considered donating them.

Detach and Discern, Then Donate!

I would rather not bring up the Achilles' heel which aptly fits in the aforementioned boots and aptly applies to my charitable consideration, but I must, as it exists for everyone hopeful of donating. The weakness, simply put, is: not everyone will want what you are willing to give them. Your life and stuff mean something entirely different to you than anyone else. For instance, I thought briefly about giving the boots to my fashionable friend, Becca, knowing she could make an outdated accessory into an amazing, on-point fashion-staple. However, when I offered them to her, she politely refused, citing a black-shoe-preference as the reason for her refusal. Maybe that was the case, or maybe she made her peace with what I hadn't. Those boots were made for walkin' and that's just what they needed to do!

This brings up another good point I always talks about when critiquing donation decisions. Having a service that will come pick up most items someone decides to part with, along with discarding them according to their direction, I've been put in more than one unique situation.

Sisters Dawn and Lisa were very happy after the Gone for Good team helped their parents relocate to a senior community

Many times, clients prefer that my team try to sell a portion of their items in a Gone for Good thrift store. Not only does it take deliberate time and effort to discern what qualifies as saleable merchandise, but it also requires discernment to consider if that is the best approach. Optimal donation considers the recipient and their need, as well as the appropriate time and way to meet their need.

Of course there are some occasions when well-intentioned people decide to donate something that has no more life, thinking, not knowing, they will meet the right need at the right time. More often than not, clothing is one of those donated items encased with the best of intentions. Cast from its owners, who still have a strange attachment, it doesn't easily or always find a new home. I hear so many misguided thoughts about clothing in particular, "These polyester suits will come back in style," customer wails. "Someone who knows patchwork would appreciate these jeans," they say. I often cautions, "One man's trash is not always another man's treasure."

When "treasure" turns into too much of a hunt and you can't find willing acceptors, it's time to consider other options. I will cover this in the next chapters. This principle applies to old and new items alike. After all, items of value may not even be accepted if personal taste and opinion differ too much. Remember when I said, when in doubt, donate? Please do so carefully.

Stephen carrying boxes

Detach from your items before you give them away. Give them to your objective help to handle handing over, the final steps required can be some of the most difficult. Decluttering experts seem to conclude many fewer items will end up with close relatives and friends than at first anticipated. Margareta Magnusson puts it this way, "You can always hope and wait for someone to want something in your home, but you cannot wait forever, and sometimes you must give cherished things away with the wish that they end up with someone who will create new memories of their own."

I once knew a woman named Claudia, who during the course of a move and downsize, tried desperately to get younger family members to value taking a theatrical wardrobe she'd accumulated over the course of her life. She said things like, "You're the same size I was at your age. If I fit into it, I would still wear it." Every attempt was made to guilt others into taking it.

Finally, someone with courage in the family said, "Claudia, I think you should donate the pieces to the local theatre company. They appreciate the life in those pieces, what they've done and what they can do." Reluctantly, Claudia agreed, murmuring and clutching a garment, "Don't you remember the time I wore this in the town's biggest production in years?" Here's a hard truth Magnusson acquaints us with all throughout her book and something we witness time and time again performing massive moves, "Your memories and your family's memories are not always the same."

There is no greater explanation for the expanding phenomena occurring in which elderly people who pass in their homes unintentionally cannot pass anything along to their next-of-kin. Let me explain. When authorities notify next-of-kin, often out-of-state, they immediately contact Gone for Good or services like ours. They do not wish to claim what's been left. Instead, they want the home cleared, sold, and out of their hands as soon as possible. Their life, with their own memories, exist elsewhere.

Bestow Like a Pro!

Refusing boots or theatrical garb is one thing—no harm, no foul—refusing something more valuable, like a home and its contents, is quite another. Damage to relationships occurs when the family doesn't accept something another finds valuable or when they aren't considered for something that is. Either way, we must refer back to chapter 4 and emphasize the importance of being aware of relational dynamics and how your decision influences them.

Once you realize the value something has to you, contain it. In fact, Margaret Magnusson suggests creating a box (something we've coined a 'death box'), marking it 'Throw Away After', and then filling it as you reminisce about the past. It's less painful

> "Before I put any pictures in an album, I usually discard multiple photos at once, simply because they are bad or because you or other people look completely crazy."
>
> —Margareta Magnusson

if you decide the relevance of certain things but never have to witness the removal. You will mainly encounter this with documents and photos, things that are not frequently donated and often appreciated solely by one party.

On the rare occasion these items are donated, they require the same discernment required for filling a 'death box.' It's important to care for these items, and process them with the same carefulness as any others. Take this on with a bit of courage and humor. Magnusson had this to say about her own process:

A donation is characterized by detachment, discernment, and dare I say it, downright honesty with yourself. Donating enables you to determine the ultimate recipient. Gone For Good can take the lead on your organization matters; or empower you to make your own discoveries. Either way, we encourage you to circulate life and charity and bestow like a pro! ❖

CHAPTER 6:

Resurrecting Life
Though Reselling & Recycling

At this point, you've determined that stuff can be a real problem. It's what to do with that stuff that many are grappling with; regardless, we must address it and decide what to do with it during the removal process. If donating isn't your avenue of choice, at least the intent of donation resonates with you. Goodwill, in any context, means having a more global, outward perspective rather than an individual, inward perspective. If donating isn't happening, it's only natural to ask and conclude:

Questions:

- What happens to the stuff I can't donate?
- What if my stuff still has enough life and value to be sold?
- What if the items could be restored to a more valuable state?
- What if there is no life or value left in my stuff and it shouldn't be donated. How then, do I recycle them?

Conclusion: As I try to channel my stuff in a more positive output instead of directly into landfills, I don't want to lose ground with my new perspective about where stuff goes and if that has a negative impact.

Reselling

While I presented some challenges of reselling items earlier in the book, there are still many positive aspects to it. One of the most exciting being replacing waste with money in your pocket.

Tom Szaky, the author of *Outsmart Waste* and the founder and CEO of TerraCycle, has a lot to say about the positive impact of presenting consumers with used items for sale. We increasingly introduce the idea of secondhand saturation as a key component to successful solutions for stuff because according to Szaky:

"Buying used durable goods, instead of new, saves a perfectly decent product that one person no longer needs from actually becoming garbage. It also prevents the need to make a new one. The good news is that used objects are typically durable; if they weren't they wouldn't have lasted long enough to show up on the secondhand market. Buying used is important because it avoids the need to manufacture a new object, making the environmental benefits of buying used immense compared with any other form of purchasing."

In a consumer-driven culture, you can't deny the impact your choices have when selling and buying. In essence, if you demand more product, you demand more garbage because the new will always become the old.

The fanatic shouts, "We should just stop buying stuff altogether!"

As anyone who's taken an economics class can attest, it's just not that simple. If you suddenly stop purchasing things, think of all the people who are out of jobs. On the other hand, if we tried to be more conscious purchasers, significant environmental impact would occur.

To better understand purchasing, read about westward pioneers. Lives for Americans changed dramatically from the first settlements to the land expansion of the 19th century. When settlers occupied the land in the 1800s, they lived off the land, planting and raising what they needed to survive. Purchasing was much different then than it is today. The pioneers' dwellings consisted mainly of items required for survival. The most shocking fact of all, when one of those items broke, they repaired it rather than replaced it.

The Industrial Revolution began a new age. Excitement came with the ability to access *more* and *better* but it curtailed any logical reason associated with the outcome of collecting and containing more stuff. Now, here we are in a day-and-age where purchasing is just a virtual decision away. We will make the decision to buy something new based simply on a new fad rather than necessity. Luckily, there is hope in changing this impulsive behavior and in how we get rid of the stuff when it becomes unwanted.

Using the example of home furnishings and what we personally support through our own processes, here's some tips on what the purchase process should look like. It's a hypothetical purchasing process designed to show purchasing and selling wisely from beginning to end:

- Person A spends a significant portion of time watching HGTV, inevitably deciding they need to redo their family living space.

- Person A considers dumping many of the belongings in the local dump for a fee but reconsiders after realizing that a quick fix isn't always the best fix.

- Person A separates the belongings into categories:

  - Items to be donated.
  - Items to be sold [which they accomplish through various channels—online, garage sale, and delivery to thrift stores similar to ours].
  - Items to be recycled.

While Gone for Good could have come in and accomplished these things for Person A, the important thing is they did them. Following the cycle from Person A's beginning removal to total fruition, look what happened:

- Person B didn't need a family room makeover. They needed their whole home furnished. An old, outdated couch didn't phase them in the least. They used what Person A no longer needed.

- Person C, an expert weaver, discovered a rare and valuable loom Person A wanted to sell. It was a $1,000 purchase and well worth the transaction in both the seller's and buyer's eyes.

- Mother Earth, reveled in the fact that her land was less full, her air cleaner, and her water purer.

Person A's contribution was small but meaningful, the type of action we believe is highly beneficial. Reselling is a small, meaningful step in changing how consumers consume.

Recycling

As you move through this book and move farther away from the idea of self-benefit you realize that stuff has a global impact. Uncovering the benefits of reselling, you have discovered the positive benefit of a cycle that moves in the right direction. To recap the benefits of recycling, you have to discover how to move consumption in a more beneficial direction.

While garbage is a modern idea, recycling is not. Just as we've mentioned before, earlier civilizations had to be more resourceful plagued with questions like *How can we make something last?* Szaky refers to recycling as a science, meaning Europeans had to be vigilant and precise in order to reuse melted down metal, a rare commodity in the Bronze Age (3300 BCE).

Today, we are learning the value these historic figures discovered: to recycle metals and other material is often less costly than reproducing them. Unfortunately, we are dealing

Newcomb loom from Davenport, Iowa.
Restored and resold because it still held value.

with something they didn't have to: plastic, which is the most difficult material to recycle. Plastics can be recycled, but we must keep in mind that the main component of successful recycling comes with separating the items.

Here's the tragedy though, we haven't developed anything better than single-stream recycling and consequently, most of what we mean to get recycled doesn't. Single stream recycling is the term used to explain consumer recycling systems in which glass, aluminum, paper, and plastics are combined for the sake of convenience.

Tsaky's book, *Outsmart Waste,* delves into details regarding the seven categories of plastics and how only the first two are currently recyclable. Additionally, he writes that there are many other plastics which can't be categorized and that more and more of these are being created all the time.

We'd like to share an excerpt from his chapter on separating waste. By giving you a few examples of separation quandaries, you'll understand more clearly the battle we're up against. regarding material sent to recycling centers:

> "...if you throw out a window cleaner bottle without taking off the trigger head, the entire bottle will be thrown out. Although the bottle is made from #1 (PET) plastic, which is recyclable, the trigger head is made from a variety of plastics and metals. The same goes if you throw out a shampoo bottle: the bottle, like the window cleaner, is #1, but the cap is #5. It's simply not economical to manually remove the trigger head or cap so that the bottle can be recycled, so it all ends up in the landfill."

As a society, we're left with serious questions about who is responsible for creating a better way. Should companies have to consider and accept responsibility for the cost of manufacturing items that combine materials in their product? Would the effect drive up cost for the consumer and halt eventual purchase of items altogether? Or, should the responsibility rest solely with the consumer? Should they resist any products that can't be recycled because of a complex make-up?

Here's the simple truth: we are sometimes more economically than environmentally motivated, which is why we want to shed some light on the environmental factors that influenced our book. Ready to talk garbage? ❖

The recycling round. The key component to recycling: materials must be separated

Part III:
Grandma, Waste Not, Want Not

A Positive Impact Mode
Molds a Global Perspective

CHAPTER 7:

Waste & Its Impact on Our Environment and Resources

At this point, you would be remiss if you continued to talk about the positive impact we can have on people by doing stuff with our stuff. Donating, reselling, and recycling but let's talk about what we've impacted the most, our environment. We've buried the facts about waste as far down in the ground as its actual contents, and now we have a problem older than any grandma.

Unfortunately, convincing subsequent generations to care about this aspect of waste is the greatest challenge of all. Perhaps a good-ol' fashion history lesson serves as the strongest persuasion about waste and its impact on the environment. Typically, books of a similar nature, present these facts at the beginning of their story, a good introduction, so-to-speak, to the topic at hand. However, being in this industry as long as I have, I've learned this: An idea such as cleaning out holds more relevance to a leary-downsizer when its related to self-benefit first.

I know there will be some of you who meticulously follow my early suggestion to arrive here wondering how you ever got in this conundrum in the first place. You will wonder how to avoid it in the future, not just for the safety and sanity of yourselves, but for the safety and sanity of generations to follow. Essentially, you will wonder about America's relation to consumerism and the global environment and the need for stabilization toward a brighter tomorrow.

Garbage is a Modern Idea with a Centuries-Old Beginning

Tom Szaky, Founder and CEO of TerraCycle says, "Human refuse—"garbage"—is a modern idea that arose out of our desire to chronically consume stuff that is made from ever more complex, man-made materials."

So, garbage is progressive, just as the modern economic theory of consumerism states that a constantly greater level of consumption is beneficial to the consumer. In effect, consumerism is why we have more and more stuff. Consequently, why we have more and more garbage.

Broken down plainly by economists at Mt. Holyoke College, "Since the 1800s and the Industrial Revolution the world has been consuming at a higher rate than ever. The Revolution allowed products to be available in enormous quantities for the first time in history. Because of their unheard of low costs, products were basically made available to all. This unlimited access led to the era of Mass Consumption. It soon grew to be expected that people have the latest model of the newest appliance. 'Why have the old model? The new one was more efficient'. This philosophy soon morphed into people buying newer models based on appearance rather than function, and consumption continued to grow. Since the 1950s, people everywhere on the globe have consumed more goods than the combined total of people throughout history. There are five basic stages of the consumer cycle: extraction, production, distribution, consumption, and disposal."

So, really, the most damage to the environment has happened over the last 150 years. At the earliest stages of consumerism, damage occurred when we dumped our old inventory in want or need of new. Garbage not only gained ground, quite literally, it also found home in boundless bodies of water. In fact, it wasn't until 1934 that the US Supreme Court outlawed waste abandonment in our oceans, a disposal technique that was quite common-place.

Garbage is a Current Crisis with an Unseen Ending

We wish that 1934 marked a significant change in garbage placement, but unfortunately, it didn't. Even though disposal was banned in the oceans, a quarter of our garbage still ends up there. Szaky points out that, "Our waste disposal 'solutions' thus far have resulted in the birth of the Great Pacific garbage patch—a pile of degraded plastic sludge 10 meters deep and as large as the state of Texas."

CBS News recently highlighted this patch and the pervasive problem of plastic when *60 Minutes* did a story entitled "Cleaning Up the Plastic in the Ocean." If hearing from Szaky that a quarter of our garbage ends up in the ocean still doesn't drive our waste problem home, this story will, laying out that 8 million tons of new plastic feed into our oceans every year. Boyan Slat, CEO of *The Ocean Cleanup*, is a young Dutchman who focuses solely on cleaning up the great ocean garbage patch.

When Slat began his campaign, the initial cost reached somewhere around 30 million dollars, which brings us full-circle to the very idea we presented at the beginning of this chapter: consumerism. The principles of supply and demand propelled us to where we are at now: amassed with stuff. "Basically," says Szaky, "the more supply there is, the lower the price will be; the more demand there is, the higher the price will be." The Industrial Revolution made it possible to have more for less.

Unless there is an equally radical revolution relating to garbage, a 30 million dollar clean-up campaign is only the beginning of a very expensive waste management onslaught we must fund. Slat funded his 30 million dollar campaign through impressive speeches and presentations which raised awareness and, in turn, money for his passionate pursuit to slay ocean sludge. On a much smaller scale, we fund our garbage disposal through waste management fees and taxes. The irony is, as we produce more waste it just gets more expensive to eliminate, thus defeating the law of supply and demand applicable to the mess that got us here in the first place. We pay to get rid of what we paid to acquire, and what we may soon realize is the price is more than we ever bargained for.

Garbage is a Future Foe We've Decided to Bury

If there wasn't a problem we want to deal with, we do like the ostrich—bury our head in the sand. As a culture, that's all we've done collectively. More aptly put, as a society, we've buried our heads in the sand while we've buried our waste deep in the ground where it is now producing toxic methane gas and decomposing at a very slow rate.

Szaky, our waste-wizard on the matter, sites three necessary ingredients for decomposition—sunlight, moisture, and oxygen. How do our landfills function then? First we line them with plastic [which still doesn't provide the proper barrier to prohibit leaching], and we stuff them to capacity, throwing a layer of soil down with each load in an official act of burial.

While I don't possess the scientific knowledge Sazky does, I do know that when layered below and beneath, garbage isn't exposed to enough, sunlight, moisture, or oxygen. It doesn't break down. In fact, gas is the greatest occurrence from this process. Methane gas builds up because of the poorly planned stages of landfill decomposition. Enough methane build-up can and has proven disastrous.

Once this gas leaches into our soils, rivers, and streams, there are no boundaries for how far-reaching the consequences may be, these grounds and tributaries mimicking veins in the human body, carrying whatever life-blood or poison flows throughout into the whole system. Exposure to methane is then all-encompassing, far-reaching, and, in the end, an indomitable opponent, a foe unwilling to be buried. ❖

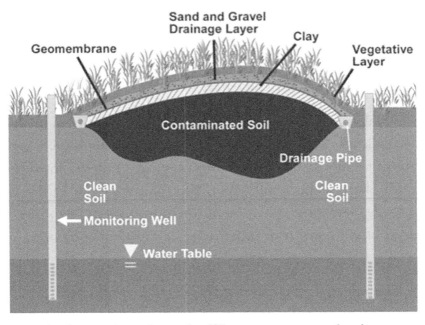

This diagram shows the way landfills contaminate our soil and water
(epa.gov/superfund/sites)

CHAPTER 8:

Less is More

If you learned anything from the last chapter it's that you can't bury your problems. Prior to that, we learned recycling stuff, despite our best intentions and uneducated assumptions, is a process that needs to grow and gain a greater momentum. You can resell some stuff, but a cultural change in consumerism would need to occur for a truly cheer-worthy result. Donation yields cheer-worthy results but not everything can be donated.

I come full circle to the very first idea I shared, **less is more.** This new paradigm for getting rid of stuff is the platform on which I founded my successful haul-away business.

Many of you reading passed this paradigm and are now trying to make less from more. Hopefully, in favor of my heartiest recommendation, you've assembled a team to help you downsize. Your team likely consists of individuals, many for whom you probably care deeply, who could benefit in laying hold of this valuable concept before they find themselves in a similar situation. In favor of them and the generations to come, we implore you to share your personal experience with stuff.

Expect the following reactions from generations which increasingly consider themselves as green:

"We've already gone green—buying resourcefully, recycling readily." We can practice 'green' all day, but it doesn't address total elimination. The fact is if we don't stop acquiring stuff in the first place, we're doomed.

Green-Colored Glasses

We're doomed because, as you'll discover in this chapter, just by the mere fact of wearing "green-colored glasses" in this society, we've given ourselves the excuse to get more. Resourcefulness cleverly disguises recklessness. Simply put, the psychology of consumerism, as it stands today, indicates that because we believe we are making environmental strides as a society, we can afford more mistakes along the way as we perfect 'Greenism.' Furthermore, as long as we're doing some things correctly, we can overlook what we're doing incorrectly.

In his book, *Junkyard Planet,* Adam Mitner shares his personal travels in the billion-dollar trash trade. You will get a sense that in this world money is the manipulator, just as I've shared all along. In a matter of mitigating this fact, companies selling tangible products conceive all kinds of "green initiatives" in an effort to blind us to this fact. Mitner sites his personal experience with Apple as a prime example.

He participated in the Apple Recycling Program and got a hefty discount on a new product by turning in his old one on the premise of providing employment to less fortunate people and refurbishing goods for less-advantaged. As he stated, who wouldn't be up for getting something better and serving others at the same time.

Mitner credits Apple as being at "the forefront of the technology industry [in] efforts to use fewer, and greener, materials in the construction of electronic devices." He felt it an added bonus that he acted on not only the most generous manner but the greenest.

So, in the end, Mitner got an upgrade, and supposedly, so did society and the environment. But the cold hard fact remains: getting rid of something is only the accumulation of something else—garbage—no matter how cleverly we downplay that fact. Sometimes we are more wasteful, simply because there's an underlying incentive to be wasteful. Sometimes, because we have come up with "green solutions," we let ourselves relax and purge relative to our perception that a positive solution occurs at the end of our transaction. Our tendency to overlook any truth related to these concepts, led Mitner to cite two terrifying experiments originally shared in the Journal of *Consumer Psychology.*

Here they are exactly as he shared them:

1. "In the first, researchers asked study participants to evaluate a new product—in this case, scissors—by cutting up paper in various, preordained configurations. Half of the study participants did the evaluation in the presence of a trash bin. The results were troubling: those who performed the task in the presence of a recycling bin used twice as much paper as those who could only throw their excess paper in a trash bin. 'This suggests that the addition of a recycling option can lead to increased resource usage,' wrote the authors, Jesse Catlin and Yitong Wan."

2. "The second experiment took place in a more natural setting: a university men's room. For fifteen days, the researchers measured the daily number of paper hand towels tossed into the trash bins positioned next to the sinks. Then they repeated the experiment by adding a recycling bin and signs indicating that certain campus restrooms were participating in a paper hand towel recycling program and that any used hand towels placed in the bin would be recycled.' After 15 days, the researchers ran the data and found that restroom visitors used approximately half a hand towel more when a recycling bin was present than when there was only a trash bin. That may not seem like much, but consider: on an average day, 100 people visited the restroom, meaning that—on average—the recycling bin (and associated signage) likely contributed to the use of an additional 50 paper hand towels per day. Extend that usage out to the 250 business days per year that the restroom is used, and in that one university restroom an additional 12,50 towels would, theoretically, be tossed into the recycling bin, annually!"

Again, what are we saying? What we are certainly not saying is that moving in a "green direction" is the wrong direction. The whole premise of our business, supported by this growing movement, launches our haul away trucks in every direction. To a recycling center, there they go! To a charitable drop-off spot, there they go! To our thrift store front for resell, there they go! What is imperative to note is how we say moving in a green direction can't be the only solution. Think back to the beginning of the chapter. In his own book, Mitner fully admitted that he didn't really need an upgrade; rather, he wanted one. Furthermore, the above experimental conclusions, drawn unbeknownst to a bunch of scissor-wielding and towel-toting people, indicate important truths about consumption and the critical need to curtail it.

Mitner shared consumption critique from the professionals who conducted the above cited-experiments:

> "'The increase of consumption found in our study may be partially due to the fact that consumers are well-informed that recycling is beneficial to the environment; however, the environmental costs of recycling (e.g.water, energy, etc. used in recycling facilities) are less salient. As such, consumers may focus only on the positive aspects of recycling and see it as a means to assuage negative emotions such as guilt that may be associated with wasting resources and/or as a way to justify increased consumption.' Elsewhere in the paper the authors add: We believe that the recycling option is more likely to function as a *get out of jail free card,* which may instead signal to consumers that it is acceptable to consume as long as they recycle the used product.'"

Our own conclusions call for our society to carefully consider how we might become more resourceful as a society and curtail consumption. How we do that might include ideas such as establishing more firm boundaries and rules for corporation and consumer alike. In the area of curtailing corporations, unleashed are a whole host of political opinions and banter that better serve a political platform. We want to serve the individual, and in turn, society as a whole by advocating boundaries. After all, boundaries never hurt anyone, particularly for those who tip the scales of excess. In fact, we as a species, can actually adapt

and produce coveted results—a more sustainable future for fellow generations—when we impose boundaries. Conversely, if we promote a flippant philosophy—At your discretion, take and use as much of a resource as deemed necessary, because in the end, we'll be able to handle everyone's personal choices— we doom our society to unknown consequences. Remember, "taking and using as much of a resource as deemed necessary" applies to accumulating as much stuff as you personally choose.

So, before you pat yourself on the back, because you never upgrade anything unless absolutely necessary or you never use more of something than you need, think about accumulation, even and only once, as a resource drain. We derived downsizing from excess. Applying the earlier-mentioned principal we conclude: getting rid of something is only the accumulation of something else—garbage—no matter how cleverly we downplay that fact. So, take off those green-colored glasses, and ask yourself, how can I acquire less, and in doing so, help more?

A Minimalistic Viewpoint

Minimalism, typically associated with decluttering, didn't originate from environmental concern. Again, in our society of self-seeking benefit, the push for this practice supports the idea that we let-loose those things which don't matter for those that do, and it's a growing trend applied to all facets of life— fashion, finance, and friendship, to name a few. Popular people like Marie Kondo, who we credited earlier for trending ideas on organization and optimal living, help elevate the idea of minimalism, citing 'joy' as a key component in deciding what to keep and what to eliminate. Testimonial after testimonial speak to her ability to help people find just that—joy—and often in doing so, create clutter-free homes that instantly get an aesthetic "face lift," as well.

Organizers caution in getting purely caught up in aesthetics, though. One such organizer, Emily Evans, founder of a professional organization company in Lexington, KY, said minimalism is so much more than making a space appealing to the eye. According to her, "If you're getting rid of stuff in your home because you're going for 'a look' or are planning to replace it with 'simpler' furniture, you're still buying into our capitalist, consumerist society," she said. "Decluttering should be about making your life easier so you can take part in things that are important to you." It's essentially saying less is more.

The Minimalists, Joshua Fields Millburn & Ryan Nicodemus, help over 20 million people live meaningful lives with less through their website, books, podcast, and documentary. On their website they speak directly to the idea of more:

"Minimalists don't focus on having less, less, less. We focus on making room for more: more time, more passion, more creativity, more experiences, more contribution, more contentment, more freedom. Clearing the clutter

Scrap metal yard, where much of the metal will never be reused

from life's path helps make that room. Minimalism is the thing that gets us past the things so we can make room for life's important things—which aren't *things* at all."

There's that idea we've been driving at all along: Things aren't the bedrock to our success. All along we've said evaluate the true value of things. Then it gets easier to see stuff for what it is—objects that, in one form or another, deplete our limited resources. To individuals these resources are space, time, money, energy, and happiness, things you can't see with the naked eye but feel deeply if your the victim of their depletion. To society as a whole, these objects which deplete our spirits, just as easily deplete more tangible resources located in the environment.

That's why, even though we appreciate in aesthetically pleasing space as much as the next person, we urge others to consider the much broader space around them. The sky above and ground below have as much to gain by our minimization as our individual homes. Additionally, joy is as important an emotion to attain as any, but let's lay hold of it for future generations as well, not just ourselves.

> ## "You have succeeded in life when all you really want is only what you really need."
>
> ### - Vernon Howard

The Message to Future Generations

Constantly considering future generations is perhaps the most careful concern we have. If we aren't concerned about what's influencing them or what they'll "buy into" next, we're not doing our part. Have you ever sat a toddler down in front of a television with the hope of silence only to be bombarded with begging for whatever is flashing on the screen in front of them? That's right—perhaps the greatest victims of consumerism are our youngest generations. Take a load of some of these startling statistics presented by the online publication, *Global Issues:*

1. Children are a captive audience: The average American child watches an estimate between 25,000 to 40,000 television commercials per year. In the UK, it is about 10,000

2. $15-17 billion is spent by companies advertising to children in the US. Over $4 billion was spent in 2009 by the fast food industry alone.

3. The marketing seems to be worth it. For example,

    ◆ Teens in the US spend around $160 billion a year

    ◆ Children (up to 11) spend around $18 billion a year

    ◆ Tweens (8-12 year olds) heavily influence more than $30 billion in other spending by parents, and 80 percent of all global brands now deploy a tween strategy.

    ◆ Children (under 12) and teens influence parental purchases totaling over $130-670 billion a year.

Our family currently lives in a modest 3 bedroom, 1400 sq. ft. home. Honestly, as parents, we could be happy here, well, forever. The fact is we have 2 kids and 1 on the way. Our teenager craves space, his 5 year old sister has enough toys to fill her own home (literally—she has a play-sized washer and dryer, mini kitchenette, and a doctor station to take care of all her many babies), and now there's going to be another child with more stuff. So what do we do? From time-to-time we discuss buying a new, bigger home to fit our increasing family amassed with stuff. As we launch our family and business forward, we start to really absorb what all that stuff is doing to the environment.

Here's the reality, we live in a media-filled world. That's not going away, neither is advertising. In fact their exposure to media and advertising will likely only increase. Currently, small children are earning huge amounts of money to present and play with certain brands on their Youtube channels in the hopes that they will expose and entice other children [or their parents] to purchase the products. On various social media platforms, people have literally been given the title of 'influencer' based on their ability to expose and promote products. We've established multi-level marketing platforms for people, convincing ourselves that a sort of "mass consumerism" is quite literally valuable to the masses.

So, with all these truths, how do we teach our kids that less is more? How can our influence become greater than the media? For those of you who purchase large homes for large families with lots of stuff, how can you positively impact future generations?

Though many are non believers, taking hold of a minimalist lifestyle, at any stage in life, is possible, even with little ones in toe. Joshua Becker, popular author, speaker, and curator of *Becoming Minimalist* reminds us of the principles his own children developed in downsizing and how they did so:

- **That we don't need to buy things to be happy.** We own far fewer things than we did years ago. We purchase far fewer things than we did years ago. Yet, we are far happier than we were years ago. Go figure.

- **That we don't need to live life like everyone else.** Even though they are not quite old enough to understand all of the intricacies of our minimalist life, they completely understand that we have made a decision to live different than most people in our neighborhood. Our lifestyle has given them permission to live a counter-cultural life.

- **That we live within our means.** Although our children are not balancing our checkbook, they do hear us speak often about debt, the joy of not being in it, and our desire to stay out of it.

- **That we think carefully about our purchases**. Because we believe in giving them ample opportunity to find/grow in their interests, we still need to buy things like toys, school supplies, art supplies, and sporting goods. We just think through our buying decisions more carefully. This is an invaluable lesson for children to learn as they get older. We no longer buy something just because we have the money, we buy things because we truly need them.

- **That we gladly share with others.** Since we became minimalist when they were young, they have grown up watching us donate many of our belongings to others. They have seen generosity in action.

- **That clutter is a drag.** They have seen how minimalism creates a home where clutter is scarce. And when it does show up, it can be quickly remedied—and usually is.

- **That we love spending time with them.** Our minimalist home has allowed us the opportunity to spend less time purchasing, cleaning, organizing, and sorting things. We have gladly replaced that time managing stuff with spending time with them.

- **That we are in control of our stuff.** Not the other way around.

So, our challenge to you, and one we're participating in ourselves, is this: start talking. Talk to your peers. Talk to generations younger than yourselves. Talk to your kids. Share the burden too much stuff caused, or is causing, in your life. Equally as important, is sharing what you're processing. Explain how as you started this book, you wanted a lifestyle lift, a way to unload a few items for a more free-filled way of living. Explain that as you unloaded, your awareness increased to include others in the project. You started realizing others could benefit through donation. Finish with the positive impacts, particularly on the environment, with decisions to resell and recycle. ❖

CHAPTER 9:

Collaboration Generation

It's the idea of influencing the following generations that's so revolutionary. When it comes to stuff, real progress is made when people work together for a common good. Nowhere else is collaboration more pivotal than in proper waste management.

By now you've learned how necessary it is to see waste for what it is and how it's impacting our environment. With that in mind, you've also learned limiting future consumption is key. The stark truth is that waste isn't disappearing anytime soon and unless communities and companies work in tandem to solve global issues relating to waste management, there won't be hope for progress. Current issues that need improvement fall under 3 categories: Contamination and Communication, Assigning the Burden to Someone, and Assuming the Burden Despite Cost.

Clear Communication: Solving Contamination

In witnessing first-hand how people recycle, we can testify to the fact that people are very confused when it comes to how they ensure recycling leaves their homes to be properly recovered and recycled. Jill Martin, a senior technical assistance specialist for The Recycling Partnership in Falls Church, VA hopes to raise the stakes for all stakeholders when it comes to the challenges of educating people about recycling.

She compared confusion surrounding recycling communication to a hypothetical break-down in transportation routes and corresponding signage:

> "Imagine trying to take a train, subway or bus system across a city where the signage, names, and colors of the routes are inconsistent. It would be difficult. But that's how many communities approach recycling education."

To better understand what's acceptable in the recycling stream at a material recovery facility, we provided the ins and outs of an established facility in Elkridge, MD below.

The facility services in the communities of Elkridge and Baltimore. Once recycling bins arrive at the local facility, employees separate true trash from recyclables as it moves down conveyor belts. By catching items that don't belong during this process, proper recycling is left behind:

"A series of spinning wheels tosses newspaper upward, leaving heavier materials to fall below. Magnets pull out metal cans, and an optical scanner detects plastic and directs puffs of air to lift milk jugs and other light containers out of the stream. Once sorted, the recyclables are pressed and tied into bales and shipped to someone who wants to turn them into something else. Much of the material heads overseas through the port of Baltimore 18 miles away."

Sounds so neat and tidy, right? Wrong. Here's where breakdown gets complicated:

"Cardboard is welcomed, but not greasy, cheesy pizza boxes. Plastic containers are OK, but if they have too much yogurt or peanut butter still inside them, they could foul an entire bale of plastics. Paper is the biggest resource, by weight, but if it's shredded and dumped into the recycling bin, it just gets stuck to glass bottles. There are other items that can be recycled, just not through single-stream sorting centers, such as plastic grocery bags, batteries and electronics. Then there are items that should go straight to the trash—garden hoses, wood pallets, or, on one recent afternoon, a bound stack of roofing shingles."

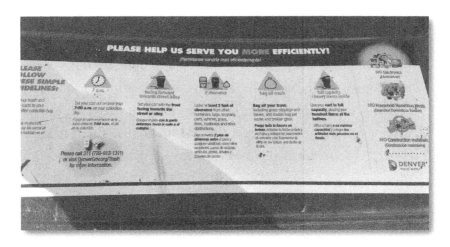

Trash collection information provided on the top of the residential collection bins in Colorado

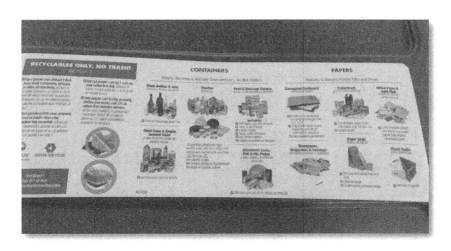

This label on top of the recycling bin explains what is and is not acceptable. While the differences seem obvious, unless the resident studies the labels it can be easy to make a mistake

America is not good at recycling. David Biderman, CEO of the trade organization Solid Waste Association of North America, attributes this to losing sight of the greatest knowledge—less is more. Biderman believes as long as blue bins are readily available and are no different than the trash bins in frame or function, Americans will inevitably use them to catch whatever doesn't fit in the other bin.

In Colorado, the recycling bins are purple

Earlier we told you that China, the lead recipient of our recycling, stopped accepting it. One of the reasons we attribute their departure from the marketplace stems from decreased need for it. The other reason is simply that America doesn't produce what they want. In essence, bad recycling makes for "contaminated" products which are less valuable and unnecessary. Even if China were still accepting the majority of America's recycling, the cost of collecting and processing recyclable materials still outweighs their value as a commodity. They can be sold back to industry for a price but not one that raises anyones' eyebrow anymore.

So, what can you do to fix contaminated recycling streams and improve recycling as a current commodity? According to Martin, Americans should keep education simple and consistent. If material recovery facilities collaborate with the communities they serve to leverage the force of media and explain what isn't acceptable in a recycling stream, community outreach could make a real impact.

Martin proposed even giving members within municipalities the opportunity to tour recovery facilities for the purpose of

"Mom, we can't take EVERYTHING to your new place at Assisted Living."

realizing how critical items like updated Acceptable Material Lists are to prevent contamination within facilities. Martin, and *The Recycling Partnership,* join communities to improve recycling systems. This is done through provisions such as a campaign-builder tool, equipped with graphics and words, for communities to utilize if funds or ideas fall short. Whether communities use this campaign building tool https://recyclingpartnership.org/PDF-BUILDER-LOGIN or create their own, communication is key in revitalizing recycling in all communities.

Even as communities move toward proper recycling awareness, a problem still exists, the cost of collecting and processing recyclable materials is greater than their value as a commodity, leaving you all to make these collaborative decisions:

1. We need to recover all recyclables more efficiently then market and sell those recovered for reuse.

2. We need to scale down on one recyclable more than any, plastic, and encourage governments and businesses to do the same.

Each realization above requires government and industry to play a major role. Communities aren't comprised solely of individual houses. Woven into each are businesses too, and government regulations play a big part in all of this.

Dual Assignment: Buying & Selling Recycling in the US

A real problem exists when mountains of recyclable material remain unsold. Recycling is a business, just like any other, and profit has to be an outcome, particularly when what is sold often can't profit enough to recover the rising cost of collection, transportation, processing, packaging, and storage.

Cardboard Baler: currently, one ton of cardboard sells for $20, which is less than it costs to pay someone to operate it for two hours.

Business and government can form an unlikely bond as they work to build industry and innovation around recyclable commodities. If government provided incentives and companies provided determination, imagine what could be accomplished! And why not? Really, it's a buyer's market for industry, as they have opportunity to acquire recyclable commodities at their lowest price to-date. It's only through them that the cycle of supply and demand will ensure a brighter future for recyclables as commodities.

As it stands, steel and aluminum are currently the only recyclables in demand. If businesses found paper and plastic recyclables to be cost-effective and consumers found paper and plastic recyclables to make high-quality products, their value would increase. Currently, while consumers may use "green" toilet paper and paper towels, they are not as aware of "green" paper and plastic products.

Geoff Davis using our cardboard crusher at the warehouse

Complications surrounding consumer confusion occur when American companies jump on the green bandwagon, their manufacturers place the chasing arrows on products, basically using it indiscriminately. As a result, sometimes the symbol means the product contains recycled material. In other instances, the symbols mean the products can be recycled and this hasn't been made clear.

The first conclusions about the green bandwagon then, is that it isn't steering you in the right direction. In some cases, it may actually be steering you in the wrong direction. These reasons are why it's so critically important for best business practices to lead the way with full support from our government.

American Airlines was one of the first to join The Buy Recycled Business Alliance, they knew that acquiring paper was a major component of business and decided it should be done more responsibly. As with most corporations, they needed to consider the bottom line and had to initiate a new way to get what they wanted for less.

Essentially, that's what it all comes down to, instituting new procurement policies for recyclable materials. Savings are achievable by making the companies' needs known to vendors and demanding competitive prices. As buyers benefit from competitive prices, they are apt to become repeat customers, guaranteeing their recyclable paper providers certain and continuous amounts of purchases. Even as businesses strive to be more responsible, you can not predict future prices and the impact of fluctuating finances of both vendor and purchaser. Therefore, responsible purchasing requires more government oversight and likely more funding, as monetary or tax incentives might entice more businesses to get green.

Environmental Concern: Prevailing Over Plastic & Price

Even as we learn ways to entice businesses to "go green," there are some already doing it because it is in the best interest of us all. Furthermore, because they make decisions based on betterment for the planet and not necessarily for the bottom-line, they see one recyclable, plastic, as a much bigger problem than as just a recyclable that isn't selling.

The irony of plastic is that it's the recyclable that's been around for the least amount of time. Created only 70 years ago, plastic has become the material with the greatest impact. During this short amount of time, humanity has produced 9 billion tons of it. While Europe recycles 30% of its plastic contribution, the US only recycles 9% of what it produces.

Such alarming statistics require companies to step up and take lead in this crisis, again, not for monetary gain but for our society's future. One such company, Macrebur, mixes recycled plastic pellets with asphalt to pave roads built to last. They laid down the first ever of such roads in the US at the University of California in San Diego. Toby McCartney, Macrebur's Managing Director, argues that his company's mixture is top-notch because it incorporates asphalt, rather than despite it. Plastic, as our statistics point out, is the ever-enduring material. Where more is more desirable to put down than on roads!

As if roads aren't innovative enough, another example of

Plastic recycling at the warehouse

major change, supported by government and business alike, occurred in Seattle where, last July, they banned plastic straws. They did so after realizing most small plastics are unrecoverable, falling through the cracks of sorting systems because of their size.

Businesses based in Seattle would be the first among its population to admit the ban wasn't necessarily easy to accept. Bob Donegan, president of Ivan's Fish Bar, a popular Seattle staple running for more than 80 years, says his company buys close to 1 million compostable straws a year despite the cost of them. After the ban, he bought compostable straws early in bulk to cut costs, but he says that's not the bottom line. Seattle citizens, his customers, demanded something better for the environment.

Another Seattle business, Taco Time, was on the forefront with Ivan's, even taking it a bit farther. According to Wes Benson, their sustainability manager, everything they use, from utensils to dishes to trash liners is 100% compostable. It costs Taco Time 5 times more to outfit their restaurant with these environmentally-friendly items, but he too sees a much bigger payoff in time.

Without companies like these two, current research shows that by 2050 there will be more plastic in the ocean than fish. Hopefully, companies continue to grow in innovation with profits that correspond to their efforts. It's almost a given that companies will need to make sacrifices. In such instances, governments could supplement losses in some capacity. Even if they can't, we all need to team up and make changes so future generations aren't drowning in plastic-plugged oceans made from today's bad choices. ❖

Part IV:
Coming Clean with Grandma

Concluding the Process
Creates Meaningful Change

CHAPTER 10:

The Gone for Good Process

After reading the last chapter, you may have a tough time getting this out of your head, people swimming in oceans of plastic. As you imagine someone frantic to swim out of the great deluge, you remember how inundated with stuff the home you're tasked with cleaning out is. Essentially, you're drowning, and you will. Unless you make the choice to complete the daunting project you began, your frantic feelings and actions will hinder any real meaningful change you need to make.

My book, carefully crammed with the 'how to's' and 'why to's,' provides information. You are the only one who can provide action, which is why we urge you to remember why you began this process in the first place. Remember how you wanted to unload a few items for a more free-filled way of living, and by doing so, help others simultaneously? These positive impacts, along with ones to the environment, enticed you to read this book. Now, through reading the book, we hope the knowledge of these three pursuits, which occur subsequently throughout the process, propel you forward to completion:

- **Start,** even if discardal, at the beginning, seems purely self-consuming.

- **Keep going** and you will discover the benefits of discardal after such important self-reflection. Through the many avenues of discardal, you'll find out how selfless purging can be. With time your gaze will shift from yourself and your stuff to others and its impact on them.

- **Finally, finish.** Meaningful change, experienced with a degree of complexity—from one person to world-wide impact—is accomplished through meaningful resolve.

If we were in front of you, our "pep talk" or personal hand-out would read something like:

Starting Simplified

You can't mess this up as bad as you think you can. When we keep things out of sight and out of mind for too long, we rarely have any reason to keep them. So stop focusing on the gigantic mess you see and start thinking about what's unseen. That's the stuff, the buried stuff, which has turned into a problem too unreasonable not to be resolved. You've also buried stuff deep inside, emotions and feelings which are now festering and emerging throughout the process. They are really the unresolved, constructing, nurturing, and compounding influencers initiating your attachment to things. Bring the tangible and intangible to light and get rid of what weighs you down once and for all.

Keep Going, Your Things Will

After all, things are weighty—they have a presence and life-cycle all their own, one which can revolve in a way yours can't. By giving away things you don't need anymore, you enable someone else to find something they need. Remember, your life and stuff mean something entirely different to you than anyone else. That's why when you donate, always consider the recipient and their need, as well as the appropriate time and way to meet their need. If donating isn't your avenue of choice, moving forward with the intent to accomplish goodwill fuels an outward perspective and corresponding outcome strong enough to help you finish what you began. You'll start to see stuff as stuff and the well-being of others as the truly important thing to consider.

Finish, Diminish, Move On!

All the meaningless stuff is from excessive consumption. So, as you purge, resolve to live more minimalistically. The sky above and ground below have as much to gain by this as your individual home. And best yet, when it's all gone, you'll discover a move isn't the only meaningful thing you've accomplished. Now, go forth and conquer! ❖

Citations

Chapter 1

Lipp, Kathi. *Clutter Free.* Eugene, Oregon: Harvest House Publishers, 2015. Print.

Paul, Sam. *Americans Love Hoarding Junk.* United States. NY Post. December 12, 2017. Web. Accessed October 27, 2018. https://nypost.com/2017/12/12/americans-love-hoarding-junk/

Jason, *Information on Hoarding Statistics.* United States. Help for Hoarding. 2019. Web. Accessed February 19, 2019. http://www.helpforhoarding.net/information-on-hoarding-statistics/

Chapter 2

Aslett, Don. *For Packrats Only.* Pocatello, Idaho: Marsh Creek Press, 2002. Print.

Chapter 3

Aslett, Don. *For Packrats Only.* Pocatello, Idaho: Marsh Creek Press, 2002. Print.

Jantz, Gregory, Ph. D. *The Psychology Behind Hoarding.* Psychology Today, September 5, 2014. Web. Accessed November 23, 2018. https://www.psychologytoday.com/us/blog/hope-relationships/201409/the-psychology-behind-hoarding

Lipp, Kathi. *Clutter Free.* Eugene, Oregon: Harvest House Publishers, 2015. Print.

Chapter 4

Magnusson, Margareta. *The Gentle Art of Swedish Death Cleaning*. New York, NY: Scriber, 2018. 7, 22-25. Print.

Chapter 5

White, Dana K. *Decluttering at the Speed of Life*. Nashville, TN: W. Publishing, 2018. 40-46. Print.

Magnusson, Margareta. *The Gentle Art of Swedish Death Cleaning*. New York, NY: Scriber, 2018. 35-36, 83, 85 & 90. Print.

Chapter 6

Szaky, Tom. *Outsmart Waste*. San Francisco, CA: Barrett-Koehlar Publishers, 2014. 24-26, 37, 53, 94-103, 113-115. Print.

Chapter 7

Gavshon, Michael. *60 Minutes: Cleaning up the Plastic in the Ocean*. CBS News, 2019. Web. Accessed January 12, 2019. https://www.cbsnews.com/video/the-great-pacific-garbage-patch-cleaning-up-the-plastic-in-the-ocean-60-minutes

History of American Consumerism. Mount Holyoke College. Web. Accessed January 12, 2019. *https://www.mtholyoke.edu/~kelle20m/classweb/wp/page2.html*

Szaky, Tom. *Outsmart Waste*. San Francisco, CA: Barrett-Koehlar Publishers, 2014. 10, 45-55. Print.

Chapter 8

Mitner, Adam. *Junkyard Planet*. New York, NY: Bloomsbury Press, 2013. 250-252. Print.

Dastagir, Alia E. *Marie Kondo, decluttering, and the war being waged against your stuff.* USAToday.com, January 9, 2019. Web. Accessed January 23, 2019. https://www.usatoday.com/story/news/2018/02/08/theres-war-your-stuff-should-you-fight/1061030001

Shah, Anup. *Children as Consumers.* Global Issues Social, Political, Economic and Environmental Issues That Affect Us All, November 21, 2010. Web. Accessed January 26, 2019. http://www.globalissues.org/article/237/children-as-consumers

Becker, Joshua. *How to Become a Minimalist with Children.* Becoming Minimalist. Web. Accessed January 26, 2019. https://www.becomingminimalist.com/how-to-become-minimalist-with-children

Millburn Fields, Joshua & Nicodemus, Ryan. *The Minimalists.* About. Web. Accessed January 23, 2019. https://www.theminimalists.com

Chapter 9

Nawaz, Amna. *Why it will take more than basic recycling to cut back plastic.* PBS News Hour, September 26, 2018. Web. Accessed January 31, 2019. https://www.youtube.com/watch?v=vCs8iZFKzdE

Biddle, David. *Recycling for Profit: The New Green Frontier.* The Harvard Business Review, November-December 1993. Web. Accessed January 31, 2019. https://hbr.org/1993/11recycling-for-profit-the-new-green-business-frontier

Martin, Jill. *Harmonized Recycling.* Recycling Today, January 2019: Volume 57/Number 1. Print.

Dance, Scott. *People are throwing too much garbage in the blue bin—and it's upending the economics of recycling.* The Baltimore Sun, January 2019. Web. Accessed January 28, 2019. https://www.baltimoresun.com/news/maryland/environment/bs-md-recycling-20180618-story.html

Companies Cited

Chapter 1

ClosetMaid—Closet organizers

Chapter 6

Terra Cycle—An Innovative and Global Recycling Company that makes typically non-recyclable waste recyclable in over twenty-four countries around the world.

Chapter 9

The Recycling Partnership, Falls Church, VA—A national nonprofit that works with communities across America to improve recycling systems. The nonprofit does this through:

1. Increasing access to recycling primarily through financial assistance for infrastructure, such as purchasing automated carts and

2. Optimizing recycling programs with technical assistance, with a large focus on cleaning up the recycling stream though things such as anti-contamination projects.

Made in the USA
Las Vegas, NV
06 February 2022

43332356R00075